West Sussex
Edited by Annabel Cook

 Young**Writers**

First published in Great Britain in 2007 by:
Young Writers
Remus House
Coltsfoot Drive
Peterborough
PE2 9JX
Telephone: 01733 890066
Website: www.youngwriters.co.uk

SB ISBN 978-1 84431 231 3

Foreword

Young Writers was established in 1991 and has been passionately devoted to the promotion of reading and writing in children and young adults ever since. The quest continues today. Young Writers remains as committed to the nurturing of poetic and literary talent as ever.

This year's Young Writers competition has proven as vibrant and dynamic as ever and we are delighted to present a showcase of the best poetry from across the UK and in some cases overseas. Each poem has been selected from a wealth of *Little Laureates* entries before ultimately being published in this, our sixteenth primary school poetry series.

Once again, we have been supremely impressed by the overall quality of the entries we have received. The imagination, energy and creativity which has gone into each young writer's entry made choosing the poems a challenging and often difficult but ultimately hugely rewarding task - the general high standard of the work submitted ensured this opportunity to bring their poetry to a larger appreciative audience.

We sincerely hope you are pleased with this final collection and that you will enjoy *Little Laureates West Sussex* for many years to come.

Contents

Liberty Clegg (8)	39
Jessica Martin (7)	40
Bethany Hayward (8)	41
Sam Jones (9)	42
Kelly Clarke (10)	44
George Yates (10)	45
Bryony Trip-Edden (10)	46
Ashley Bingham	47
Nathan Riley (8)	48
Harvey Clarke (8)	49
Bethany Tetley (8)	50
Harry Kelly (8)	51
Kieran Quinlan (8)	52
Emily Drake (7)	53
Joseph Miller (8)	54
Kai Shield (8)	55
Adam Shimell (8)	56
Joshua Simmonds (8)	57
Georgia Deane (8)	58
Sophie Kelly (8)	59
Joe Jones (8)	60
James Harris (7)	61
Emily Ray (7)	62
Toby Lauder (8)	63
Rebecca Williamson (7)	64
Hollie Belcher (8)	65
Harvey Robinson (10)	66
Tod Sinclair (10)	67
Kiera Ashman (10)	68
Robert Napper (9)	69
Alice Bennett (10)	70
Melissa Ayers (10)	71
Sarah Millyard (10)	72
Harry Jandula (10)	73
Abigail Smith (9)	74
Oliver Cooper (10)	75
Daniel Riley (10)	76

Bosham CP School, Bosham

Joe Duncan-Duggal (10)	77
Katie Maslen (10)	78

Hannah Taylor (10)	79
George Bell (10)	80
Kate Oldfield (10)	81
Georgia Beckingsale (10)	82
Sophie Bishop (10)	83
Jessica Illman (10)	84
Oliver Nightingale (10)	85
Emily Redstone (10)	86
Frances Carruthers (10)	87
Imogen Stockman (10)	88
Oliver Holley-Williams (10)	89
Holly Guest (10)	90
Megan Wickins (10)	91
Harry Colley (10)	92
Harry Sarjant (10)	93
Georgia Vessey (10)	94
Matthew Bennison (9)	95
Lara Andrews (10)	96

Great Ballard School, Nr Chichester

Elise Kearsey (7)	97
Elise Kings (8)	98
Ben Olofson (8)	99
Leah Constantine (8)	100
Ralph Pauling (8)	101
Ian C Richardson (10)	102
Daniel Shlosberg (9)	103
Wolf Labeij (9)	104
Tassia Cloran (10)	105
Daniel Shlosberg (9)	106
Tasha Dahya (10)	107
Jemima Spurr (8)	108

St John's RC Primary School, Horsham

Lydia Evans (7)	109
Neil O'Rourke (8)	110
Callum Oldmeadow (8)	111
Aoife Simm (7)	112
George Carbone (8)	113
Emily Jacob (8)	114
Ciara Berkeley (8)	115

St Joseph's Catholic Primary School, Haywards Heath

James Massey (11)	155
Lily Greene (9)	156
Nathan Foley (8)	157
Alexander Zbinden (7)	158
Tom Burnell (8)	159
Lara Antoine (8)	160
Phoebe Tuckett (8)	161
Charlie Kelly (8)	162
Harry Thompson (10)	163
David Warde (9)	164
Isabel Beauchamp (11)	165
Sebastian Blunt (9)	166
Thomas Blunt (9)	167
Joshua Furminger (10)	168

Tangmere CP School, Tangmere

Jacob Tice (11)	169
Dominic May (10)	170
Alana Misselbrook (10)	171
Chloe Robinson (10)	172
Abbie Warrior (10)	173
Eve Osborne (10)	174
Emma Hanson (11)	175
Melissa Killick (11)	176
Melissa Hills (10)	177
Bradley Dean (10)	178
Nicola Frisby (10)	179
Emily Clifton (10)	180
Chloe Albuery (10)	181
Danielle Foster (11)	182
Matthew Hart (10)	183
Leah Acott (11)	184
Oliver Rutter (10)	185
Tiffany Hudson (10)	186

The Prebendal School, Chichester

Emily Hill (10)	187
Edward Walker (10)	188
Polly Tyerman (9)	189
Harry Dry (11)	190
Luciana Macari (11)	191

The Poems

What Happened That Night?

He was walking in the night
He could hear footsteps
But not his.
The sound of footsteps got closer and closer,
He turned, no one was there,
But when he turned back . . .
There was silence,
And how it surged softly backwards.
He screamed
And was never seen again.
What happened that night?
What was out there?
Something.
Is it still out there now?
We'll never know.

Ruth Byrne (10)
Bishop Tufnell Junior School, Bognor Regis

Earthquake

I was sitting there in silence.
I felt a tremor,
I looked outside but everything seemed fine.
There it was again.
I jumped up, put my coat on
And ran outside without looking.

Argh! I was falling,
The wind was taking my breath away.
I had butterflies in my stomach.
Before I knew it, I was in a different world,
A strange world,
I had never been here before.

There were people dressed in rags
And dogs with no fur,
The road was a ribbon of moonlight
As bright as a bolt of lightning.

Siobhan Rogers (10)
Bishop Tufnell Junior School, Bognor Regis

They Were There

The night was as dark as coal,
He felt like he was being followed.
The trees and bushes were rustling,
They heard his fear.
He was shivering like ice was touching his bare skin.
He shouted, 'Help! Help! Help!'
But still no answer, just the sound of owls hooting.
He ran,
They followed . . .
He was getting paranoid.
He fell on the floor shouting, 'Help! Help! Help!'
But nobody was there,
Only a host of phantom listeners
To listen to his every scream . . .

He ran into the forest,
As he stood there, still as a rock,
He knew they were there.
The man was going crazy.
They were there,
Their eyes staring right at him.
'Help! Help! Help!' he shouted.
They came closer . . .
He needed a way out.
His legs were like spaghetti,
Shaking like jelly,
But as they came closer
He tried to run,
But he was surrounded by them,
They were like a brick wall.
One leaped out to touch him
But as it did,
He gently fell to death.

Sam McAlpine (10)
Bishop Tufnell Junior School, Bognor Regis

Anger

Anger is black like a child in a train of horror.
Anger looks like a big dark hole.
Anger tastes like a rotten lemon.
Anger smells like some from a fierce fire.
Anger reminds me of the dark,
Anger sounds like the scream of a dying lady.
Anger feels like being stabbed.

George Cleall (8)
Bishop Tufnell Junior School, Bognor Regis

The Footsteps

It was cold that night.
A man was there, he could hear footsteps,
They were coming, they were moving,
                   Click-clack, click-clack.
He didn't know what was going on, he was scared.
It was coming closer, he ran behind an old broken tree,
He looked up, the sky was as dark as coal.
They were louder,
                   Click-clack, click-clack.
He stopped on the spot, he screamed,
It was a monster, it was a ghost monster.
He was curious, he was screaming, 'Help!'
The monster was on a chariot.
The man was running,
The chariot ran over him,
Blood and bones burst out.
The chariot just went riding, riding.

David Crouch (10)
Bishop Tufnell Junior School, Bognor Regis

Anger

Anger is red like a volcano,
It looks like a big, red flaming fire,
It smells like a flaming bonfire crackling in the night,
It feels like a rough bear walking in the woods,
It tastes like a sour lemon,
It reminds me of fighting with my sister,
It sounds like thunder rumbling in the dark sky.

Jack Freeburn (8)
Bishop Tufnell Junior School, Bognor Regis

Love

Love is red like a heart,
It feels like a river flowing,
It smells like roses in a pot,
It tastes like peppermint creams,
It looks like a heart,
It reminds me of people who look after me,
It sounds like a chocolate fountain flowing like a waterfall.

Hannah Halliday (8)
Bishop Tufnell Junior School, Bognor Regis

Sadness

Sadness is blue like waves crashing on the sand,
It reminds me of wind blowing in the sky.
It sounds like dolphins jumping over the waves,
It smells like clouds in the sky,
It tastes like a river,
It looks like an ocean.

Chelsie-Leigh Hewitt-Ward (8)
Bishop Tufnell Junior School, Bognor Regis

Fear

Fear is the colour red, like a werewolf's shining red eyes,
It sounds like a big volcano erupting,
It looks like a boiling cauldron full of red water, full of people's fears,
It smells like a different place,
It feels like a tight rope in my tummy,
It reminds me of lightning cracking outside my bedroom window,
It tastes like a boiling cup of tea.

Daniella Matthews (8)
Bishop Tufnell Junior School, Bognor Regis

Sadness

The colour of sadness is blue.
Sadness reminds me of someone upset.
It tastes like tears,
It sounds like it's upsetting,
It smells like salt,
It feels like I broke a toy,
It looks like a clown face.

Dominic Humphries (8)
Bishop Tufnell Junior School, Bognor Regis

Love

Love is pink like rose petals in the wind,
It smells like candyfloss,
It feels like a soft breeze in the sky,
It looks like people holding hands.
Love tastes like lovehearts going down your throat,
It reminds me of the sea going to the horizon,
It sounds like music at a wedding.

Kathryn McKrill (7)
Bishop Tufnell Junior School, Bognor Regis

Sadness

Sadness is white like the fluffy clouds,
It reminds me of a scary ghost,
It smells like smelly petrol,
It tastes like plain, ready salted crisps,
It sounds like barging footsteps,
It looks like a tear going down someone's face,
It feels like your heart beating very fast.

Maisie Mountain (8)
Bishop Tufnell Junior School, Bognor Regis

Sadness

Sadness is brown like a dark wood,
It smells like a rotting body,
It reminds me of a graveyard and sad music at a funeral,
It feels like slime all over you,
It looks like a relative dying in front of you,
It tastes like a rotting apple.

Charlie Davies (8)
Bishop Tufnell Junior School, Bognor Regis

Love

Love is red because of your heart,
It sounds like a tweeting bird in the summer,
It looks like a family hugging to say goodbye,
It tastes like melted chocolate, hot in your mouth,
It smells like lavender after washing your clothes,
It feels like lying in on a Sunday morning,
It reminds me of having my first best friend.

Georgia Crisp-Mills (8)
Bishop Tufnell Junior School, Bognor Regis

Love

Love is red like a red rose,
It feels like the fluffiest cat you have ever seen,
It looks like the reddest rose you could ever see,
It tastes like ice cream,
It smells like a rose,
It reminds me of my mum and dad,
It sounds like birds tweeting.

Daniel Hind (7)
Bishop Tufnell Junior School, Bognor Regis

Hate

Hate is grey like the wind blowing in the air,
It tastes like the toast in the toaster,
It sounds like a bird singing in the sky,
It feels like the soft fur of a dog,
It looks like a really tall tree,
It smells like the water in a swimming pool,
It reminds me of the horrible creatures in the wild.

George Bingham (8)
Bishop Tufnell Junior School, Bognor Regis

Love

Love is as red as a rose.
Love feels as warm as a fire.
Love looks peaceful and nice, just like the calm wind.
Love reminds me of doves flying gracefully through the air.
Love smells like nature and wildlife.
Love tastes like warm, fluffy, cooked cookies.
Love sounds like baby chicks tweeting in the morning.

Caitlin Jones (8)
Bishop Tufnell Junior School, Bognor Regis

Hate

Hate is black like a stormy sky,
It tastes like carrots,
It smells like fish being cooked,
It sounds like screaming,
It looks like someone hitting another person,
It feels like squidgy play dough,
It reminds me of being angry.

Gemma Hawker (8)
Bishop Tufnell Junior School, Bognor Regis

Happiness

Happiness is yellow like sand on a seashore,
It smells like roses,
It tastes like spaghetti Bolognese,
It looks like children playing on a beach,
It reminds me of my family in the park.
It sounds like people laughing,
It feels like a smooth dog.

Claire Lomax (8)
Bishop Tufnell Junior School, Bognor Regis

Sadness

Sadness is blue like the wavy sea,
It feels like soft, silky silk,
It tastes like freezing cold ice in the snow,
It looks like the wind blowing side to side,
It smells like chocolate in the shops,
It sounds like people crying,
It reminds me of falling to the ground.

Jenna Goose (7)
Bishop Tufnell Junior School, Bognor Regis

Happiness

Happiness is blue like the calm sea,
It reminds me of a sunset in the sky,
It sounds like a trumpet,
It feels like ice cream on your tongue,
It looks like a marshmallow,
It tastes like an apple,
It smells like my favourite dinner.

Myles Garrett (8)
Bishop Tufnell Junior School, Bognor Regis

Fear

Fear is black like a spider, all tickly,
It smells like rotten cabbage,
It tastes like glue, all slobbery,
It sounds like thunder on a stormy night,
It looks like a flat spider bleeding,
It reminds me of a dark room with flies and spiders.

Ben Askew (7)
Bishop Tufnell Junior School, Bognor Regis

Anger

Anger is green like dark mountains,
It smells like blood,
It tastes like rotten apples,
It sounds like screaming,
It looks like dark shadows,
It reminds me of death.

Michael Donnelly (7)
Bishop Tufnell Junior School, Bognor Regis

Sadness

Sadness is blue like tears dripping down your face,
It feels like a flood of raindrops,
It tastes like rotten apples,
It smells like rotten vegetables,
It looks like crashing waves on the beach,
It sounds like someone crying.
Sadness reminds me of a bucket of onions.

Joshua Edwards (8)
Bishop Tufnell Junior School, Bognor Regis

Anger

Anger is red like boiling fire.
Anger smells like smoky fire.
Anger feels like a steaming kettle.
Anger tastes like peppers.
Anger looks like flames.
Anger reminds me of an exploding volcano.
Anger sounds like stamping on a wooden floor.

Conah Lambe (8)
Bishop Tufnell Junior School, Bognor Regis

Sadness

Sadness is white like tears dropping down your face,
It feels like a water fountain,
It tastes like water,
It smells like ice,
It reminds me of a waterfall,
It sounds like a calm river,
It looks like someone with tears on their face.

Nicole Embleton (8)
Bishop Tufnell Junior School, Bognor Regis

Fear

Fear is blue like a dark volcano.
Fear smells like rotten cheese.
Fear tastes like rotten apples, disgusting, revolting food.
Fear looks like a broken-down tree.
Fear sounds like a falling mountain that goes on forever.
Fear reminds me of when people are very unhappy.
Fear feels bumpy and hard.

Michael Hurst (8)
Bishop Tufnell Junior School, Bognor Regis

Hate

Hate is grey on a very stormy night.
Hate sounds like an angry volcano.
Hate feels like a broken heart.
Hate tastes like a rotten apple.
Hate looks like an angry person.
Hate smells like some rotten vegetables.
Hate reminds me of a big scary monster.

Jack Quiroga (7)
Bishop Tufnell Junior School, Bognor Regis

Anger

Anger is red like a flower in the daylight,
It reminds me of a volcano erupting,
It feels like frustration,
It tastes like blood,
It looks like rough and tumble,
It smells of rotten vegetables,
It sounds like thunder on a stormy night.

Tommi Nagle (7)
Bishop Tufnell Junior School, Bognor Regis

Happiness

Happiness is yellow like the boiling yellow sun,
It smells like a sweet-smelling rose,
It sounds like birds chirping in a tree,
It looks like people smiling in the street,
It tastes like the best food you've ever tried,
It reminds me of my holidays in Florida,
It feels like smooth pebbles on the beach.

Mitchell Cane (8)
Bishop Tufnell Junior School, Bognor Regis

Anger

Anger is red like an exploding volcano.
Anger tastes like red-hot lava burning in my mouth.
Anger is like a million clouds falling on you.
Anger feels like rain is following you.
Anger looks like a black hole sucking you up.
Anger smells like a flicker of a fire.
Anger sounds like thunder and lightning ripping the sky.

Scott Bingham (8)
Bishop Tufnell Junior School, Bognor Regis

Happiness

Happiness is like a beautiful fluttering butterfly.
Happiness tastes like a marvellous chocolate cake.
Happiness looks like a class of smiling children.
Happiness smells like a bunch of roses.
Happiness sounds like a big twinkling star.
Happiness feels like a strand of hair.
Happiness reminds me of the best food in all of the world.

Sophie Kingdom (7)
Bishop Tufnell Junior School, Bognor Regis

Love

Love is pink like when two people hug.
Love smells like flowers opening at dawn.
Love feels like happiness.
Love tastes like strawberries in a chocolate fountain.
Love sounds like happiness forever.
It reminds me of my auntie and uncle's wedding in Florida.

Sophie Adamson (8)
Bishop Tufnell Junior School, Bognor Regis

Fear

Fear is as white as a snowy day.
Fear smells like a scary ghost.
Fear sound like a skeleton dancing in the street.
Fear feels like a skeleton's hand touching me.
Fear tastes like a disgusting cake.
Fear looks like a haunted house.
Fear reminds me of lots of very scary monsters.

Abbeygail Longhurst (7)
Bishop Tufnell Junior School, Bognor Regis

Love

Love is pink like a bouquet of flowers.
Love looks like hearts skipping across a field.
Love smells like a rose.
Love sounds like bells.
Love feels like the sun on my body.
Love tastes like sweets.
Love reminds me of a sunny day.

Alice Jarvis (7)
Bishop Tufnell Junior School, Bognor Regis

Fear

Fear is yellow like fire all around you.
Fear reminds me of a windy tornado.
Fear smells like smoke.
Fear feels like a pin being stabbed in my heart.
Fear tastes like boiling fire.
Fear looks like a ghost.
Fear sounds like a mouse.

Jamie Wilson (8)
Bishop Tufnell Junior School, Bognor Regis

Happiness

Happiness is white like the wind on a cold day.
Happiness smells like a flower floating in the sky.
Happiness feels like playing in the park.
Happiness reminds me of friends.
Happiness sounds like music with a fast beat.
Happiness looks like the sun.
Happiness tastes like chocolate.

Keir Musk (7)
Bishop Tufnell Junior School, Bognor Regis

Dumb As A Dog

His name is Dumb
Because he does not know anything.
His mum puts food in his bowl but he lays by the fire.
They all went shopping and he laid by the fire.
The doorbell rings and he lays by the fire.
He's so dumb.
He buries his bone and forgets where it is,
He's so dumb.
He chases his tail and circles around and around,
He's so dumb.
He licks his tum, he's so dumb,
But we love Dumb, the dog, he's our chum.

Grant Aldred (10)
Bishop Tufnell Junior School, Bognor Regis

Sadness

Sadness is blue like a rippling river.
Sadness tastes sour like limes in your mouth.
Sadness looks like tears splashing on the floor.
Sadness sounds like crashing waves on the beach.
Sadness reminds me of rain.
Sadness feels damp and grey.
Sadness smells like rotting food.

Liberty Clegg (8)
Bishop Tufnell Junior School, Bognor Regis

Hate

Hate is like a heart,
It feels like a person frustrated,
It smells like hot air,
It tastes like a bit of lime,
It looks like someone exploded,
It sounds like a volcano,
It reminds me that you are not a friend anymore.

Jessica Martin (7)
Bishop Tufnell Junior School, Bognor Regis

Happiness

Happiness is yellow like the sun beaming down on me.
Happiness tastes like a beautiful, delicious cake.
Happiness looks like lovely bunches of roses.
Happiness reminds me of every happy memory.
Happiness smells like lavender in a garden.
Happiness feels like a soft cuddly toy.
Happiness sounds like a bird singing in the sky.

Bethany Hayward (8)
Bishop Tufnell Junior School, Bognor Regis

The Chase

He ran further;
He was scared.
That creature;
That thing,
It freaked him.
Trees were being torn from the ground,
Deep blackness;
Freezing cold;
The sky was like coal,
But he would never give up.
Never,
Never,
Never . . .

He ran out of the deserted village
Into the forest,
But the monster didn't lose sight of him.
As he sprinted across the fluffy floor of the forest,
He realised that the thing behind him was gone.
He looked,
He stared.
Suddenly it leapt out of a bush!
The man yelled and sped towards the village.
The monster was still there,
But he would never give up.
Never,
Never,
Never . . .

He was so exhausted,
All his energy had been sapped away from him,
But he kept going . . .
He kept going on and on and on,
High-pitched screaming in his ear,
Trying not to think of the creature behind him.
He saw the animals finding it hard to survive.
He stumbled and fell.

A shadow fell over him,
This was it,
He'd lost.
It was
The end,
The end,
The end . . .

Sam Jones (9)
Bishop Tufnell Junior School, Bognor Regis

The Forest

The forest
Was deathly silent
When the man walked in.
The trees swayed softly
In the gentle blowing wind.
Slowly, the man walked on,
Then he turned.
What,
What was that sound?
Someone, something,
Was coming,
Coming with the stench,
The stench
Of old grass and rust.
The man was terrified,
The creature was still approaching.
The man ran,
The creature stopped
And how the silence surged softly backwards.
The sunrise came and the creature
Burst into flame,
But was the man still safe?
Was the creature still out there?

Kelly Clarke (10)
Bishop Tufnell Junior School, Bognor Regis

The Shadow Slayer

The fog-infested wood had been dead for long,
Everybody had come and gone.
It had been destroyed by the great storm.
The abandoned wood had some life,
In the distance a figure was sighted,
There was a shuffling through the leaves on the ground.
What was running round and round?

The man was trapped, which way did he go?
He turned and twisted, he didn't know.
How could he choose? So he stood perplexed and frozen.
Through the faint mist he could see a dark shape,
It looked like a shadow, from whom I don't know,
But it crept around and rustled the leaves.
He started to shiver, especially his knees.

The figure came, but very slow.
He pulled out a net and crouched down low,
Then he leapt and ran very fast,
He grabbed the man in his net
And left him where he was, stuck stiff,
After he jumped with all his might,
Then held the shadow very tight.

The dramatic end to the fight
Ended with a flash of light.
Then they vanished into thin air,
Maybe into the shadow slayer's lair.

George Yates (10)
Bishop Tufnell Junior School, Bognor Regis

Ice Apples In Winter

It was a windy night,
The trees frosted and bending in the wind.
The floor padded out with snow
As a little girl was walking in the dark.
Crunch, crunch, crunch.
She went, shivering and shaking,
Carrying a bag of apples from a tree,
But the weird thing was that apples
Don't grow on trees in the middle of winter.
Munch, munch, munch.
She ate an apple,
Her lips were ice, her hair was snow . . .
Blow, blow, blow,
The wind was blowing harder,
Her eyes were watering, her nose was bright and sore.
The snow was falling fast,
It melted when it touched her head.
Drip, drip, drip.
It made her head wet,
But she did not care as
She slowly disappeared that night,
That girl, that ghost . . .

Bryony Trip-Edden (10)
Bishop Tufnell Junior School, Bognor Regis

Love

Love is as red as a rose.
Love reminds me of the time when my mum and dad got married.
Love smells like a beautiful red tulip.
Love sounds like a blissful harp.
Love looks like a bag of hearts.
Love feels like a happy, loving couple.
Love tastes like red cherries.

Ashley Bingham
Bishop Tufnell Junior School, Bognor Regis

Fear

Fear is grey like volcano ash,
It sounds like cracking and crunching ground,
It feels like a worried, scared person,
It looks like annoyed werewolves,
It smells like stinky old rubbish,
It tastes like disgusting pickled onions,
It reminds me of when I fell off the edge and onto the train track.

Nathan Riley (8)
Bishop Tufnell Junior School, Bognor Regis

Hate

Hate is dark red like lava erupting,
It feels like you want to get someone back,
It looks like a roaring lion,
It reminds me of when I kick my brother,
It sounds like a growling bear,
It smells like after a fight.

Harvey Clarke (8)
Bishop Tufnell Junior School, Bognor Regis

Anger

Anger is red as a burning fire.
Anger is purple like bruises!
Anger sounds like people shouting all the time.
Anger tastes like sharp raspberries in your mouth.
Anger looks like steam coming out of someone's ears.
Anger feels like sharp claws on your body.
Anger reminds me of when I get told off.
Anger smells like hot chilli peppers in a pot.

Bethany Tetley (8)
Bishop Tufnell Junior School, Bognor Regis

Love

Love is pink like a pounding heart,
It reminds me of my caring family,
It smells like a dashing rose,
It tastes like delicious chicken,
It sounds like singing birds,
It looks like happiness,
It feels like magic.

Harry Kelly (8)
Bishop Tufnell Junior School, Bognor Regis

Fear

Fear is black like a howling wolf,
It smells like burning wood and a smoky fire,
It reminds me of when I was scared of the costumes on Hallowe'en,
It tastes like a sour lemon,
It sounds like a lion roaring,
It feels like a panther killing its prey,
It looks like a raging killer whale.

Kieran Quinlan (8)
Bishop Tufnell Junior School, Bognor Regis

Happiness

Happiness is yellow like a sunny day,
It smells like a burning campfire,
It sounds like a laughing child,
It reminds me of when my brother is nice to me,
It tastes like sweet strawberries,
It feels like a soft pillow,
It looks like a Christmas party.

Emily Drake (7)
Bishop Tufnell Junior School, Bognor Regis

Anger

Anger is dark red like an erupting fire,
It reminds me of when people didn't let me play football,
It sounds like frustrating music,
It feels like hot, burning lava,
It looks like a horrible devil,
It smells like a sizzling golden sun,
It tastes like when I have to eat Brussels sprouts.

Joseph Miller (8)
Bishop Tufnell Junior School, Bognor Regis

Hate

Hate is dark black like a raging bull,
It feels like bolting thunder,
It tastes sour and bitter,
It smells like smoky fire,
It looks like a roaring lion,
It reminds me of when I shouted at my sisters.

Kai Shield (8)
Bishop Tufnell Junior School, Bognor Regis

Sadness

Sadness is blue like a freezing cold winter,
It reminds me of when I broke my arm,
It looks like a big red spot,
It reminds me of when I hurt my eyes.
It tastes like a drip of a tear,
It feels like a car running over you,
It sounds like a baby crying.

Adam Shimell (8)
Bishop Tufnell Junior School, Bognor Regis

Fear

Fear is black like coal,
It tastes like hatred,
It smells like cold air,
It looks like a vicious monster,
It reminds me of Hallowe'en,
It feels scary and frightening,
It sounds like a haunted house.

Joshua Simmonds (8)
Bishop Tufnell Junior School, Bognor Regis

Happiness

Happiness is gold like the big shining sun,
It smells like a bright pink tulip,
It tastes like a bowl of sweet cherries,
It reminds me of my best friend, Holly,
It sounds like a small bird chirping,
It feels like a soft kitten's fur,
It looks like a colourful rainbow.

Georgia Deane (8)
Bishop Tufnell Junior School, Bognor Regis

Hate

Hate is grey like an elephant.
Hate feels like when my brother shouts at me.
Hate smells like burning wood.
Hate looks like someone upset.
Hate reminds me of my sister crying in the wind.
Hate sounds like a person who is disappointed.
Hate taste like someone who is very *mad!*

Sophie Kelly (8)
Bishop Tufnell Junior School, Bognor Regis

Sadness

Sadness is dark blue,
It feels like an angry tiger leaping on you,
It tastes like sour lemon,
It sounds like sad funeral music,
It reminds me of when I broke my toe,
It looks like a blue tear,
It smells like a burning fire.

Joe Jones (8)
Bishop Tufnell Junior School, Bognor Regis

Hate

Hate is dark red like a fiery devil,
It looks like a fierce shark,
It smells like a hot red fire,
It tastes like hot spicy chillies,
It reminds me of when I kicked my dog,
It sounds like a lion roaring,
It feels like when you're furious.

James Harris (7)
Bishop Tufnell Junior School, Bognor Regis

Love

Love is as pink as a beautiful flower,
It sounds like a pounding heartbeat,
It tastes like a delicious wedding cake,
It smells like a red rose,
It looks like a caring family,
It reminds me of my colourful budgie,
It feels like a romantic film.

Emily Ray (7)
Bishop Tufnell Junior School, Bognor Regis

Anger

Anger is black like thunder,
It reminds me of when I saw a sandstorm in Cyprus,
It sounds like a loud bang,
It feels like a hot fire,
It looks like a dangerous fight,
It reminds me of when I kicked my brother in the jaw
                                        on my trampoline,
It tastes like burning rubber.

Toby Lauder (8)
Bishop Tufnell Junior School, Bognor Regis

Love

Love is red like a bright pink rose,
It sounds like beautiful, romantic music,
It reminds me of when I fell over in a rosebush and my mum
                                                    took care of me,
It smells like Cadbury's milk chocolate,
It looks like two people getting married,
It feels like a happy, loving couple.

Rebecca Williamson (7)
Bishop Tufnell Junior School, Bognor Regis

Happiness

Happiness is red like a rose,
It reminds me of playing with my best friends,
It tastes like a box of yummy chocolates,
It sounds like joyful music,
It feels like jumping over the moon,
It looks like two doves in love,
It smells like a delicious cake.

Hollie Belcher (8)
Bishop Tufnell Junior School, Bognor Regis

Nowhere Street

Five men were chuckling way out at sea,
Non-stop sailing that was heading towards a storm.
Hell ahead,
And so shipwrecks everywhere to see.
Some old gentle breeze shot across,
Then a new power jet of frost and hail,
Shaken and worn on this world.
'Land ahoy!' is what Captain would say,
So quiet, so quiet, though it was for long.

All around complete silence
As they stood on sand and concrete.
Clatter,
It sounds like a horse,
It called from the knight in armour,
It snuck towards the bunch of men,
Led them to a moor.
Clatter,
It will not stop,
It cannot stop,
It is riding to the sun and the moon,
All men watching then behind to see a great big wood . . .

Seems as though we've left that town,
The street from out of the blue,
We can tell our Earth, of our world;
Pure drivel,
One small problem in our way,
Lost,
This wood is really petrifying,
Fishermen fall for evermore
In this wood called Foxen Forest and the suburbs of
                                        Nowhere Street.

Harvey Robinson (10)
Bishop Tufnell Junior School, Bognor Regis

The Bus Stop

At the sacred woods showing over the wicked wonderland
Shines a dull line of gleaming tall trees.

Far in amidst the dust sways a road in mist
And a grey gang of people that they had missed
Sneaking by terrified past what they called 'The Bus Stop'
They're all frightened . . .

Seconds later starts a swampy super storm
Dark tragically falling tremendously,
Like the wind was a torrent of darkness
In the gorging, skidding sky, past the soggy dust within the fog
It fuses, whooshes past with the gang from 'The Bus Stop'
They're all frightened . . .

Now they feel lost for life; no hope to be found
But in that jungle, one had been vanished up into a magical cloud
Finding the sight of a weird, silent, screeching voice
Now everybody's soul is burning
With wicked fear and fright
Every boy's soul is broken and those people are vanishing
They're all frightened . . .

There is only one man left
Standing completely perplexed and still
Begging and shouting from his soul
'Help!' he screamed, and again, 'Help!'
But the jungle was coming to life so he ran
But his heat and soul inside just couldn't take it
When he stopped, he found a cliff in front of him
And lit from his heart
They're all frightened . . .

Rising over that cloudy cliff, there were the others looking mutated
But with a flash taking the others circling around him
Instantly 'The Bus Stop' takes him with it
Back to where it began by fluke!

Tod Sinclair (10)
Bishop Tufnell Junior School, Bognor Regis

Fox In Winter!

The trees were swaying,
The wind whistling,
A little fox was sleeping,
Then it woke.
It heard the faint sound of a squeaking gate,
It followed it.
It plodded through the moss and mud
And finally came to a silver gate.
It slowly crept towards it and saw a hint of sparkle.
This time it ran,
It flung the gate open and . . .
Trees with bronze bark,
Crystal droplets hanging from the leaves,
Snow as soft and fluffy as ever.
The road was a ribbon of moonlight
Twisting, turning, winding.
It plodded through the fluffy snow
And found amazing things.
For the rest of its life it lived there,
And an amazing life it lived.

Kiera Ashman (10)
Bishop Tufnell Junior School, Bognor Regis

The Mysterious Man

In the woods on a dark, damp day,
A mysterious man walks slowly past the swaying trees
With a dull black cloak from his head to his knees.
His hood is over his head,
He's quieter than a mouse.
An owl flies out of a tree squawking.
Everything is quiet on the dull, damp day . . .

The man keeps on walking through the dull, damp woods,
His black cloak keeps swaying in the strong wind.
He hears a shadow rustle in the bushes behind him,
He is frightened.
He tries to flee but he is frozen with fear.
The thing crawls out of the shadows,
It growls at the man and . . .

They will never forget that day,
With the full moon shining down upon them.
There was blood everywhere on the trees, on the bark,
The only thing left was a skeleton on the ground.

Robert Napper (9)
Bishop Tufnell Junior School, Bognor Regis

Snakes Of The Night

The man stood there frozen to the spot,
His fiery hair shining in the moonlight,
His cheeks glowing orange, his lips as red as roses.
He'd heard a noise behind him, behind him;
A slithering sound amongst the grass.
He turned around, shivering with fright.

But there was nothing there, except
The old rotten trees and the peculiar musty smell . . .
He suddenly called out in pain as
The snake sank his teeth into the man's leg.
There was silence . . .
As the man fell to the floor in agony;
His leg was swollen and bleeding.

The snake passed the man, hissing and spitting,
And then disappeared.
The wind turned frozen all of a sudden,
But soon became its cool breeze again.
The frozen winds came again, came again;
But this time they said something,
'We are the crystal-clear snakes of the night
Wrapping ourselves around the wind.'
All was silent . . .
Nobody ever knew where the man went.

Alice Bennett (10)
Bishop Tufnell Junior School, Bognor Regis

Spirits

In a clearing there stood two spirits
Of girls who had died that misty day.
They stood there watching, listening,
For someone to come by.
The girls were waiting for anything to happen.
They watched the moon as it sailed across the sky.
The moon looked as though it were a ship
Skimming across the waves of night.
The little girls told each other in ghostly whispers
That the moon had never looked so calm,
Yet so ghostly before.

Years passed before anyone entered that wood.
Those girls were missed in the village.
Someone came looking for them,
Who was it?
The girls were so happy.
They waved their arms and shouted,
But the man walked through them!
'Hello,' he called.
Silence!
'Not here I guess,' he said, walking away.

The girls cried and cried until they couldn't cry another tear.
If you look in that wood when the moon is full,
They're still there, lying in wait for someone . . .

Melissa Ayers (10)
Bishop Tufnell Junior School, Bognor Regis

The Dusty Road

The night was cold and quiet
Along the dusty road
Until a man in a coat of claret velvet
And breeches of brown skin
Came running along the dusty road.
The wind was rough but I stood there
Brave and still.
The man came running to me . . .
I was scared, scared of the man that was running . . .

The man came closer . . .
The wind got rougher . . .
I got frightened, scared, terrified.

The dust on the road was blinding as it blew along
The road,
The cold, cold, dusty road.

Sarah Millyard (10)
Bishop Tufnell Junior School, Bognor Regis

The Jungle Battlefield

He was walking through the jungle,
His patrol's weapons at the ready;
The enemy were searching for him,
For he had just destroyed a train which carried ammunition,
So the explosion was louder than a sonic boom.
There was a rustle behind them,
They turned around,
A bird flew out of a turret; then rifle fire shot out.
His patrol ran, even though their supplies and
Ammunition slowed them down.
A few stayed and fought,
The rest of the patrol got away,
But the part that fought all fell where they stood.

He was scared to death,
He didn't know who was going next.
He didn't know when the next attack would come.
When suddenly it came, it was a complete bloodbath!
Guns blazing on both sides!
He was constantly reloading his Tommy gun!
His patrol was constantly losing numbers!
At the end of the battle there were casualties on both sides.
It was disgusting; bodies everywhere
And pools of blood on the floor.

There were fifteen people left out of the seventy-five sent out!
There was a huge amount of casualties.
He had some minor injuries
But could still walk.
Most of his friends were dead,
But they had succeeded!
They were heading home!

Harry Jandula (10)
Bishop Tufnell Junior School, Bognor Regis

This Creature Of Some Sort

She walked through the cold, gloomy woods;
Not an animal in sight . . .
Or person . . .
She heard some footsteps, footsteps, footsteps,
She turned but no one was there . . .

She carried on walking. She heard footsteps again.
She turned but no one was there, so she walked a little faster,
But she still heard the footsteps.

She turned, but this time she screamed.

She carried on screaming, but this creature of some sort
Stayed put.

His eyes were hollows of madness, his hair like mouldy hay,
His nose was like a rotten carrot,
And she was scared.

She stopped screaming and ran,
But this creature of some sort jumped in front of her.
She went to run the other way,
But this creature of some sort grabbed her!

She shouted for help,
But no one came to help the sweet, little, innocent girl.

So she was never seen again!

Abigail Smith (9)
Bishop Tufnell Junior School, Bognor Regis

The Dark Night Sky

In the dark night sky . . .
In the dark woods . . .
Beyond the rotting trees,
His feet felt heavy, really heavy.
The moon was shining brighter than a flame.
He walked, limping.
His hair was like mouldy hay,
His eyes were hollows of madness.
The air was as cold as ice.
He was the only one in the woods that night, that night,
As the trees swayed from side to side
And as wolves hollered and howled.
But no one knows what happened to that man that night,
That night while the wolves hollered and howled.

Oliver Cooper (10)
Bishop Tufnell Junior School, Bognor Regis

Always Stay With Someone In The Woods

It was a dark winter's night,
The wind was a torrent of darkness,
Everything was as black as coal
And he came running . . .
Running . . .
Running, looking for his friends.
He kept on running . . .
Running . . .
Running, even though
He was scared to death inside.
Then it came . . .
It came . . .
It came, the master of them all.

He had blue eyes,
A creamy coat
And miraculous grey trousers.
He had a long stick in his right hand
And a knife in his left.
He dropped his stick,
He grabbed him
And took him to his camp.
No one knows what happened to him.
Is he dead?
Is he still in the woods?
No one knows . . .
No one knows . . .
No one knows.

Daniel Riley (10)
Bishop Tufnell Junior School, Bognor Regis

Manchester United!

Man U is the team for me,
Winning the cup they look glorious!
So glorious it makes Chelsea envious!
Our style is luxurious!
Man U are just so fabulous!

Chelsea's skill is atrocious
And Arsenal look ridiculous
Compared to our gracefulness!
We will prove it when you watch us play,
With Rooney being vicious
And scoring loads of goals!

Joe Duncan-Duggal (10)
Bosham CP School, Bosham

My Cat

I have a cat called Mars,
I suppose he is hilarious.
I push him in a baby pram,
I think he is quite glorious.
I hold him like a baby
And make him feel quite serious.
He lays on my bed at night,
I think he is anonymous.

Katie Maslen (10)
Bosham CP School, Bosham

Me And My Art

Art is the thing for me,
All of it's spectaculous.
My pencil sits there on the table,
I'm really being serious,
And all the things I draw and paint,
So many think ridiculous,
But most of the things I'm telling you
Are very, very obvious . . .
That one simple line I draw
Will get so very famous,
And because I get so very oblivious,
Lots of things go wrong.

Hannah Taylor (10)
Bosham CP School, Bosham

My Dog

My dog is the best in the world,
It makes my friends quite envious.
He licks everyone he meets,
It's really quite hilarious.
He daydreams sometimes,
I think he's quite delirious.
When he's done something bad,
It really is quite obvious.
He's a bit silly sometimes,
He can be quite ridiculous.

George Bell (10)
Bosham CP School, Bosham

I Love My Dog

I love my dog, she makes me laugh,
I think she thinks she's fabulous.
I think she really is.
I love my dog, she is so cute,
But she can be rather mischievous.
I love my dog and I think
She loves me too.

Kate Oldfield (10)
Bosham CP School, Bosham

Cheetah

I am a cheetah,
As marvellous as I can be,
Furious and feisty, I can be,
So don't follow me.
I am dangerous, so sleek and sly,
I may sound outrageous,
But I am really quite delicious.

Georgia Beckingsale (10)
Bosham CP School, Bosham

Gymnastics

I love gym,
Every time I go, I do the splits,
And it makes my friends very envious.
When I'm older, I might be famous.
My friends think I'm joking,
But I'm being serious,
And it makes me furious.

Sophie Bishop (10)
Bosham CP School, Bosham

My Hamster!

My hamster is cute and
She makes my friends so envious.
But really I am serious
That my hamster is a genius
As she is good at doing things.
She's so glorious,
She thinks her tricks are obvious,
But other hamsters think it's laborious,
And some hamsters think it's hilarious,
But my hamster's fabulous.

Jessica Illman (10)
Bosham CP School, Bosham

My Cat

I have a cat called Midge,
Who is very small,
He looks like he's eaten a tennis ball.
He has a brother called Mungo,
Who is goofy and he is hilarious.

Oliver Nightingale (10)
Bosham CP School, Bosham

My Cat, Tango

My cat called Tango is very bouncy,
She really is hilarious.
Sometimes she scratches me,
Then I get quite serious.
She is very cute and
She really looks mysterious.
She likes her food very much,
She thinks it is nutritious.

Emily Redstone (10)
Bosham CP School, Bosham

Art

I love to draw and paint,
It makes me quite delirious,
Though some of my art is not so good,
Some of it is fabulous.
Animals are the best to sketch,
'N' drawin' cats is glorious,
Now it may sound like I'm boastin'
But I really am a genius.
There is nothing quite so great
As art, it is luxurious.
One day I can see
I will be really famous.

Frances Carruthers (10)
Bosham CP School, Bosham

My Fish

My fish, he swims quite fast,
He says he really thinks he's fabulous.
What I think about my fish, I really think he's mysterious.
My fish says that I'm not mad because I say he's hilarious.
When people come to look at my fish, they all say he's hideous.
The good thing about my fish is that I think he's glorious,
Even though people say he's very, very ridiculous.
I could just wish that my fish was very, very famous.
I've just realised that my fish is quite spontaneous.

Imogen Stockman (10)
Bosham CP School, Bosham

Mobile Phones

I like mobile phones,
I think they are fabulous.
The buttons are shiny
And very glorious.
I am proud of the man who invented them,
I think he is very famous.
I think their invention was genius.
The ringtones can be very luxurious.
They come in different types and they are hilarious.
I love my mobile phones, they make me delirious.

Oliver Holley-Williams (10)
Bosham CP School, Bosham

Climbing

I like climbing, it's my thing,
To me it's quite luxurious.
When I get to the top,
I feel rather glorious.
You may think going up and down
Is quite ridiculous,
But you are wrong for thinking that,
In fact it's quite incredulous.
You may think I get delirious
Being at that height,
But going up there so many times,
I feel quite fabulous.
I should have turned your thoughts around
About this genius sport.
So why not try it?
It might be fun,
For it is not ridiculous.

Holly Guest (10)
Bosham CP School, Bosham

My Dogs

I have two dogs called Rocky and Daisy,
They make me feel quite glorious.
Rocky makes my friends quite curious,
Because he's so mysterious.
Daisy is quite glamorous,
As she's quite notorious.
All my friends get jealous
Because of my wonderful dogs.

Megan Wickins (10)
Bosham CP School, Bosham

Tennis

Tennis is a brilliant game,
It is really fabulous.
When you win it's even better
And it makes you feel delirious.
But when you lose it's very sad,
And you find the game ridiculous.
When it's down to the last point, it's really tense,
And you feel quite anxious.

Harry Colley (10)
Bosham CP School, Bosham

Football

I think football is the best,
It is fun 'n' furious.
Players slide and hack you out,
I s'pose it's quite ridiculous.
Before a match you don't know who
Is going to win or lose,
I find it quite mysterious.
The ref is annoying,
But he is so serious.
When players get a red card,
It is so hilarious.

Harry Sarjant (10)
Bosham CP School, Bosham

Drawing

Drawing is so beautiful,
I think I am a genius.
Most people think it is ridiculous,
But they are *so* wrong.
You probably think I'm stupid,
But I'm really being serious.
When people say I'm bad,
I get so very furious.
I can get quite scary,
You could call me vicious,
But when I rub out,
Everything becomes oblivious.
When my friends come round,
They say I'm spectaculous.

Georgia Vessey (10)
Bosham CP School, Bosham

Cricket

Cricket is a wicked game,
Some people say it's serious,
Others say it's ridiculous,
It makes me act delirious.
When you win it's brilliant,
Excellent and glorious,
But when you lose it's really sad,
It makes you feel atrocious.
When you're going in to bat,
You're feeling very nervous.
It's hard to hit a six because
The pitch is so enormous.
In-between you and the boundaries,
It's looking very spacious.

Matthew Bennison (9)
Bosham CP School, Bosham

Dancing

I am a dancing queen,
It makes me feel fabulous.
My styles are tap and modern,
And it makes my life glorious.

I love my dancing very much,
Because I'm becoming victorious.
I am now on grade three
And my mum says I'm supercalifragilisticexpialidocious!

Lara Andrews (10)
Bosham CP School, Bosham

Jack Frost

Jack Frost was in the garden,
I saw him there, I did!
He was dancing and prancing,
I didn't know where to look.
He danced and pranced all over,
And ran and jumped the fence.
He flew over the field
Like a glittering bird,
Then he flew back to Heaven.

Elise Kearsey (7)
Great Ballard School, Nr Chichester

My Pet

My pet is not soft or furry,
Or one you can teach tricks.
It is slimy and slithers and hisses.
Called Killer, he chomps on flesh.
His fangs attack the bones.
Who would not want this cute little pet?
It's a snake!

Elise Kings (8)
Great Ballard School, Nr Chichester

Counting

1, 2, 3, 4, 5, once I caught a shark alive.
6, 7, 8, 9, 10, then I threw him back again.
Why did you set him free?
Because he started eating me!
From which section did he eat?
From my neck down to my feet.

Ben Olofson (8)
Great Ballard School, Nr Chichester

Woof!

Woof! Woof! The dog's on the move,
Kicking and scratching
And being a pain!
His name is
Chocolate
And he's
Dark brown,
Very small,
And three years old.
He's very cute and
He's very cuddly,
And also handsome.
Oh!
And did I mention the owner?
Well, the owner!
The *owner!*

Leah Constantine (8)
Great Ballard School, Nr Chichester

Bugs

Beautiful butterflies sitting on a bright flower,
Ugly woodlice in a box,
Gruesome dung beetles pushing cow pats,
Silly, funny worms slithering about,
Some beautiful and ugly bugs we saw.
Then my friend squashed them all.
Oh no!

Ralph Pauling (8)
Great Ballard School, Nr Chichester

The World's Destruction

When Heaven falls and Atlantis sinks,
And the nose falls from the mighty Sphinx,
Evil creatures will rise once more,
To forever feast on living gore.
Once the exiled of Stonehenge,
Now they come to seek revenge.
Bloodthirsty monsters with power immense,
Their foes are left without defence.
Giant engines of chaos and war,
Their hunger is for evermore.
Living off our very own souls,
They drag us into their portholes.
Then our flesh is ripped by claw,
Now they start to eat it raw.
Their awesome feast is never through,
Could you be their victim too?

Ian C Richardson (10)
Great Ballard School, Nr Chichester

My Dad

My dad's an alien hunter,
He always says, 'Watch your back.'
Then I tell him there's no such thing as aliens,
He disappears at that.

He thinks his duty is to save the world,
Although he's a dustbin man,
He searches through the rubbish,
Then he's in his van.

When he finds a phone number,
He texts, 'I come in peace.'
Then the person replies,
'Who are you? I'm calling the police.'

So there you have it,
My dad, the silliest person on Earth.
I always give him a Star Trek wave
On the day of his birth.

Daniel Shlosberg (9)
Great Ballard School, Nr Chichester

Night-Time - Haiku

Telling jokes in bed,
Laughing in the winter night,
Having lots of fun.

Wolf Labeij (9)
Great Ballard School, Nr Chichester

Nintendo DS Mario Bros Game - Haiku

In goes the game - *jump!*
Quick, get the giant mushroom.
Yes, super big *win!*

Tassia Cloran (10)
Great Ballard School, Nr Chichester

Furious Island - Haiku

Tidal waves belting,
Volcanoes bubble and burst,
Nature is at war.

Daniel Shlosberg (9)
Great Ballard School, Nr Chichester

Snowflakes - Haiku

Snowflakes falling down
Snowball fighting round and round
Cold snow, freezing hard.

Tasha Dahya (10)
Great Ballard School, Nr Chichester

Ponies

My pony can showjump like a dream.
If you are lucky, you can get a rosette.
You have to jump one foot nine or two foot.
If you do cross-country, you could get a trophy.
If you get a moon and a star, you get a medal.

Jemima Spurr (8)
Great Ballard School, Nr Chichester

My Planet

In some other galaxy there could be a fantasy world
With marshmallows growing on trees.
Next to the trees there is a beautiful lake
With sparkly blue water flowing down to a white, soapy waterfall.
In the waterfall there are pink and blue aliens
With white fluffy wings washing themselves.
The other aliens are making houses.
Candy grows from the floor and if you eat it it grows back!
I am the best planet of all.

Lydia Evans (7)
St John's RC Primary School, Horsham

Azbaldon

I am Azbaldon, a friendly planet.
I defend myself from enemies.
I am 8 billion miles away from Earth.
I have golden lakes of fish, the fish swim slowly through.
I keep every abandoned person who goes on me.
I have colourful rings and I am turquoise.

Neil O'Rourke (8)
St John's RC Primary School, Horsham

Snow-Po-Co

Snow-Po-Co is my planet.
The robots are as fascinating as science.
The snow is stormy and cold.
It has spaceships that are as flat as a pancake
And as fast as lightning.
The base is as big as a giant.

Callum Oldmeadow (8)
St John's RC Primary School, Horsham

Candy Land

My planet is Candy Land.
Sherbet snow falls beneath the candy.
Little chocolate people live on Candy Land.
My planet is like a cute pink balloon flying by.
An icy lolly ring circles around it.
Pretty little flowers pop up every minute.
Millions of chocolate mountains grow on the surface.
It has sparkly rainbows flying by every day.
If you eat Candy Land it grows back again.
Everything on my planet is pink.
My planet is delicious!

Aoife Simm (7)
St John's RC Primary School, Horsham

Planet Plutus

Every year the sun passes by.
The planet Plutus changes colour.
It is a marble rolling across the sky.
Crystals blazing bright.
It's cold.
Blazing bright strikes.
Every person who goes there never returns.

George Carbone (8)
St John's RC Primary School, Horsham

Planet Saturn!

Saturn's rings are as frosty as ice.
It glows so brightly as it spins around its moons.
Saturn is round and very, very quiet as it floats in space.
Saturn's colours are bright yellow and pale cream.
It is as peaceful as quiet music.
It has beautiful stripes on it.

Emily Jacob (8)
St John's RC Primary School, Horsham

Venus

My planet is more golden than the sun.
My planet is more glitzy than the stars.
My planet is like a lamp in a dark room.
My planet is as warm as a mother's love.
My planet is a glowing marble in the night sky.
My planet is exciting because it's mine.

Ciara Berkeley (8)
St John's RC Primary School, Horsham

Planet Chocy

My planet is made of chocolate.
It is dripping with caramel and toffee.
The core is made of candyfloss.
If people land on it their feet sink.
If it gets too hot it melts and has a flood.

Josie Perkins (8)
St John's RC Primary School, Horsham

My Planet Arthur

I'm a lifeless warrior in the night
As fierce as King Arthur
I have a golden coat of sunlight
I have a spiky surface with a sandy floor
I am half water half fire
I fling fireballs everywhere from my volcano
I look after any human who comes on me
I wear a belt
I have a broken sword of iron.

Declan Gorton (8)
St John's RC Primary School, Horsham

Space Is Coming

I was frozen cold, I could see the sun.
I was near a volcano,
It started to explode with lava
And lighting is coming soon.
I have to leave.
Can I find my way back to Earth?

Conor Gibson (7)
St John's RC Primary School, Horsham

My Planet Icicles

My planet is sky-blue like the sky.
Snow-white like snowflakes.
Daffodil-yellow like the sun.
Moon-grey like the moon.
As peaceful and quiet like a library.
The surface is solid like a rock.
See-through like glass too.

Marlie Wint (8)
St John's RC Primary School, Horsham

Black Planet?

There are diamonds and crystals,
It is cold on one side but boiling on the other.
Diamonds flashing in the black sky,
The rocks are made of types of jewels.

Joseph Burke (7)
St John's RC Primary School, Horsham

Planet Fudge

It's gummy it's yummy.
It's so delicious you just want to eat it all up.
There are fudge mountains.
It is very peaceful.
When you step on it you will not feel a thing.
Take a big bite. Wouldn't that be a treat?

Shea Taylor (8)
St John's RC Primary School, Horsham

My Planet Trily

My planet rolls like a shimmering marble in the starry night sky
sparkling with a pure blue lake
where golden fish swim gracefully
silver crystals dotted around beachy palm trees
cheeky monkeys swing tree to tree.

Ali Carter (7)
St John's RC Primary School, Horsham

Green Trident

Astronauts come from far and wide.
It's easy to smell the fruity breeze.
At Trident's mountain tops the planet glows bright green when
                                        the sun goes down.
A blue lake on the surface that sparkles crystal blue.
The sand is just like grains of sun sprinkled everywhere.
All you can hear from galaxies away is Trident's lake crashing
                                        on the rocks.

Martha Haste (8)
St John's RC Primary School, Horsham

Safrina

I'm the best of them all and the biggest.
I'm a dazzling sight to any human being.
I'm beautiful, everyone bows down to me, even my friend Jupiter.
I'm what looks like a smiling face from miles away.
I'm the Queen.

Mary Hurst (8)
St John's RC Primary School, Horsham

Planet Of The Toffees!

Look at me so special like a diamond
I am yummy and delicious
A planet called Planet of The Toffees
Where you can find aliens, candyfloss and gardens of sweets
Aliens made of fudge, plates made of a chocolate bar
With sugar mountains and fountains of milk from milk lakes.

Abigail Ann Brooks (8)
St John's RC Primary School, Horsham

My Planet

It has golden sand rocks.
It has life just like us.
It has a cosy atmosphere.
It has a lovely ocean.
It has cosy countries.

Hector O'Donnell (8)
St John's RC Primary School, Horsham

The Lifeless Planet Venus

An orange lonely marble rolling in the dark blue sky.
The core is a lifeless golden ball.
Its mysteries lie within its core.
This planet is Venus.

Niall Chapman (8)
St John's RC Primary School, Horsham

Lonely

Like a lost lamb in a field on his own with no mother
eating a blade of grass at a time.
Its wool is as soft as smooth feathers on a bird
perching on a tree in the rainforest.

Gemma Fraser (9)
St Joseph's Catholic Primary School, Haywards Heath

Anger

Anger
It is that feeling when you get frustrated
Anger
Your face goes really red
Anger
You want to shout at someone
Anger
You get really frustrated
Anger
Wanting to explode.

Jake Henry (9)
St Joseph's Catholic Primary School, Haywards Heath

Anger

I feel angry when people annoy me
My heart beats fast
My head explodes with anger
I feel angry.

Jules Chasteauneuf (9)
St Joseph's Catholic Primary School, Haywards Heath

Worried

I can feel my mind filling up to the top,
going to overflow.
I can feel my heart thumping out of my skin
like an animal wanting to get out.
I feel like I've done something wrong.
I feel all shy.
I feel all lonely like an abandoned lamb
all alone in one big field.

Esther Pattman (9)
St Joseph's Catholic Primary School, Haywards Heath

As Worried

As worried as a mother trying to protect her young.
As worried as when you break something that you can't replace.
As worried as when you get told off by the head teacher.
As worried as when your dog's just eaten your homework.
As worried as a lost lamb.
As worried as being stuck up a tree.
As worried as if a big hairy tarantula was crawling up your back.
As worried as when you're at the top of a roller coaster hill.
As worried as if you were in the sea and a shark started to
                                        swim towards you.

Alice Burke (9)
St Joseph's Catholic Primary School, Haywards Heath

Darkness

Darkness is black, like coal burning in a fire,
It reminds me of a never-ending tunnel where there is no light,
Where there is no hope,
It feels like you're in a cage with a rug thrown over it,
Where there is light outside but no light inside,
It smells like a burning candle which is nearly out,
It tastes like a rotten carrot which you are scared to touch,
Which you are scared to go into,
It sounds like a beggar begging for money,
It sounds like a woman shrieking for help as she gets tortured,
Darkness looks like a murderer stabbing someone a million times.

Hugo Tuckett (10)
St Joseph's Catholic Primary School, Haywards Heath

Fear

Fear is black like the Devil's cloak,
Fear is cold like a dead body,
Fear tastes like blood,
Fear smells like death,
Fear reminds me of being in a cage with a jaguar,
Fear sounds like someone screaming.

Kieran Edwards (10)
St Joseph's Catholic Primary School, Haywards Heath

Anger!

Bubbling and frothing, angry snake ready to strike.
Fizzing and flying, red-faced teacher at boiling point.
Punching and kicking, bullies close in on me.
Run away, feet burning, feet on fire.
Stretching and pulling, stitch in my side.
Stop, breathe, stop, breathe, quickly, fast,
All is calm, walk home, fire still burning inside me.
Need to hurt, need to kill, need to fight urge!
Pick up stone, throw, sound of splintering glass,
Broken window, person hurt, run away, into bullies!

Emily Rose Eckford (10)
St Joseph's Catholic Primary School, Haywards Heath

Stress

When I never get listened to,
Stress,
When things are broken and you can't replace them,
Stress,
When someone is annoying you and they always win,
Stress,
When time runs out and you can't carry on,
Stress,
When you get told off for not doing anything,
Stress,
When there are two different choices,
Stress,
I let it all out!
Stress!

Ellen Kenrick (10)
St Joseph's Catholic Primary School, Haywards Heath

Silence . . .

Silence feels like a shivering person crying for help,
Silence sounds like someone dying in a cold night,
Silence smells like dirty dust and a gone-off coffee,
Silence reminds me of a slow death gradually building,
Silence tastes like blood from my own body,
Silence looks like a cold fog with no one in sight,
Silence is as painful as watching paint dry.

Ciaran O'Connor (11)
St Joseph's Catholic Primary School, Haywards Heath

Fear

Fear is red like blood oozing from a woman.
It tastes like death in a coffin.
It sounds like silence in an empty graveyard.
It looks like murder with a knife.
It smells like blood, fresh from a man.
It feels like fire burning on you.
Fear reminds me of someone screaming.

Alex Covey (11)
St Joseph's Catholic Primary School, Haywards Heath

Silence

Silence is grey, duller than dull.
It tastes like metal, hard and tough.
It feels like a never-ending nightmare.
It smells like chalk, boring and uninteresting.
It looks like mountains, lifeless and lonely.
It sounds better than the atmosphere at Stamford Bridge.
Silence reminds you of death!

Jez Rodriguez Badell (11)
St Joseph's Catholic Primary School, Haywards Heath

Laughter

Laughter is yellow as the sun,
It smells of melting chocolate,
It feels like happy memories,
It reminds people of hope,
It looks like a colourful parade,
It tastes of cool ice cream.
Laughter sounds of the ever-blowing wind.

James Symons (11)
St Joseph's Catholic Primary School, Haywards Heath

A Poem Of Fun

Fun is bright yellow like the warming sun,
It is a wonderful feeling inside you,
It tastes like candy poppers in your mouth,
It sounds like children on a roller coaster,
It smells like a sweet shop, all the delicious fizzy sweets,
It reminds me of a happy holiday in Spain,
Fun looks like playing on the beach.

Xavier Nicholls (11)
St Joseph's Catholic Primary School, Haywards Heath

A Poem Of Fun!

Fun is yellow like the sun,
It feels like something buzzing inside you,
It tastes like candy poppers, popping in your mouth,
It sounds like children playing in the park with their friends,
It smells like a sweet shop, lovely and sweet,
It reminds me of a holiday in Walt Disneyland,
Fun looks like children having fun on a bouncy castle.

Joseph Donohue (11)
St Joseph's Catholic Primary School, Haywards Heath

Happy

I feel happy like the sun on a hot day
And a child seeing someone that you have not seen in a long time.
Happy as a group of children playing together.
I feel so happy my heart could jump out.
I am so happy like the school will be closing down.

Charlie Ghosh (10)
St Joseph's Catholic Primary School, Haywards Heath

Anger

Lightning coming out of my ears,
The volcanoes erupt and even the stormiest of seas can't put
                                                          them out,
Earthquakes crushing the ground behind my back,
I feel like everyone and everything is against me, like nobody is
                                                          on my side.
There is no hope, just that burning feeling inside.

Ciaran Crawford (10)
St Joseph's Catholic Primary School, Haywards Heath

A Poem Of Fear

Fear is the colour of dark red blood oozing out from a deep fresh cut,
It feels as though you are being eaten inside your small heart,
It sounds like darkness dooming you for the rest of your long life,
It smells like a large, red, putrid rotten apple slowly decaying,
It reminds me of red blood trickling down my beautiful face
When a large, strong bully hits me as hard as possible,
It tastes like drinking your own warm sweat when you are scared stiff,
It looks like you are watching yourself suffer a long, horrible death,
Fear is like you wish you had never been born in a beautiful world!

Luis Walters (10)
St Joseph's Catholic Primary School, Haywards Heath

Hunger

Hunger is green like a new leaf on a tree,
It sounds like a rumbling stomach,
It smells like roast beef cooking on a hot stove,
It reminds me of poverty in Africa,
It tastes of really sour lemons,
It feels like emptiness,
Hunger looks like a skinny child.

William Hazelwood (10)
St Joseph's Catholic Primary School, Haywards Heath

Fun

Fun is a colourful bright rainbow,
It feels like stroking the deep crystal ocean,
It sounds like children running around laughing happily,
It smells like a mountain of different coloured roses,
It reminds me of a day out to the beach,
It tastes like 'Toxic Waste',
Fun looks like glistening sea when the sun strikes on it.

Eleanor Baxter-Smith (10)
St Joseph's Catholic Primary School, Haywards Heath

Happiness

Happiness looks like a rainbow of bright, bold colours.
It reminds me of my fun football tournament.
It tastes of melting chocolate.
It looks like friendship.
It feels like never-ending life.
It smells like fragrant flowers.
Happiness is joy.

Joshua Keay (10)
St Joseph's Catholic Primary School, Haywards Heath

Laughter

Laughter is as colourful as the rainbow.
It smells like a delicious chocolate ice cream.
It sounds like the happiness of a child.
It looks like someone is having fun.
It reminds me of being young.
It feels like going down a roller coaster.
Laughter tastes like a great fry-up.

Kyle Barter (10)
St Joseph's Catholic Primary School, Haywards Heath

Gentle

As gentle as a mother
singing her baby a lullaby.
As gentle as a soft feather
landing on a soft cub's wet sparkling nose.
As gentle as a smooth ripple
in the middle of a calm deserted river.
As gentle as a spider's web
blowing in the wind.

Annie-Rose Donohue (10)
St Joseph's Catholic Primary School, Haywards Heath

Laughter

Laughter feels like a comfy pillow,
It is yellow like a gleaming sun,
It tastes like nice, sweet Dolly Mix,
It sounds like a lively theme park,
It looks like loads of brightly coloured bouncing balls,
It reminds me of The Dolphin Fair,
Laughter smells of the midsummer breeze.

Sarah Jane Mendes (10)
St Joseph's Catholic Primary School, Haywards Heath

Angry

As angry as a lion.
As angry as a football team losing a match.
As angry as angry could be.
As angry as a volcano killing everything in its path
And everyone in its path.
As angry as a hen whose chicks have been taken away.
When teachers blame you for something you have not done.
When your friends make a big deal of something you did not
                                        know you did.
When someone really makes you angry.

Antonio John (10)
St Joseph's Catholic Primary School, Haywards Heath

Lonely

When I am lonely I feel like an abandoned chick,
When I am lonely I feel like the soft breeze rushing through the air,
When I am lonely I feel like dust getting blown through the desert,
When I am lonely I feel like a soldier in a war that has survived,
When I am lonely I feel like the last leaf in the freezing winter,
When I am lonely I am *sad*.

Jordan Burge (10)
St Joseph's Catholic Primary School, Haywards Heath

Arrows

Bow sends arrow flying
Point kills an enemy
Wood carved so well
Points as sharp as claws
Ostrich fur so soft
Hunter is pleased he has killed his prey.

Conor Froud (9)
St Joseph's Catholic Primary School, Haywards Heath

Laughter

Laughter is yellow like the bright burning sun
It feels as soft as a baby's bottom
It sounds like children playing joyfully in a warm swimming pool
It smells like a bunch of fresh scented roses
It reminds me of happy, fun ski holidays in France
It tastes like sweet, fresh strawberries with a teaspoon of sugar
Laughter looks like someone enjoying themselves at the beach.

James Massey (11)
St Joseph's Catholic Primary School, Haywards Heath

Quickly

Quickly the chocolate horse trots over the dusty wasteland,
Quickly the spotted cheetah zoomed out of the wet jungle and
                                        into the quicksand.
Quickly the cherry-red motorbike screeches to a stop.
Quickly a fast racing car wins the lot.
Quick is the waterfall, but quickest of all is the yellow, fast cheetah
                                        creeping in the hall.

Lily Greene (9)
St Joseph's Catholic Primary School, Haywards Heath

Quickly

Quickly the hare lost its pace,
Quickly the racing car won the race,
Quickly the horse munched its hay,
Quickly the hare jumped away.
Quick is the waterfall but
Quickest of all is the plane, which is best of all.

Nathan Foley (8)
St Joseph's Catholic Primary School, Haywards Heath

Quickly

Quickly the horse galloped across the field neighing madly
like it was a horse roller coaster.
Quickly the cheetah ran after the scared to death hare
across the muddy field.
Quick is the hare but quicker is the sound,
But quickest of all is the light.

Alexander Zbinden (7)
St Joseph's Catholic Primary School, Haywards Heath

Quickly

Quickly the heavy plane fell on the train,
Quickly the hurt passengers got out in pain,
Quickly the fast cheetah ran after the hare,
Quickly the vicious hunters try to kill a bear,
Quickly the red racing car finishes the race,
Quickly the running man runs to Marle Place.
Quick is the rocket but quickest of all
Is the speed of sound from the old waterfall.

Tom Burnell (8)
St Joseph's Catholic Primary School, Haywards Heath

Stars

Lights shining brightly,
Shining in space,
Hundreds of lights in the sky,
Glimmering yellow floating high up.
Bright yellow points gleaming in the moonlight.

Lara Antoine (8)
St Joseph's Catholic Primary School, Haywards Heath

Quickly

Quickly the plane zooms through the sky,
Quickly the light shoots far up high.
Quickly the clouds drift through that clear space,
Quickly a fast car finishes the race.
Quickly a blue boat tips on its side,
Quickly a sandcastle is caught in the tide.
Quick is the hare, but quickest of all
Is the shining blue water in the waterfall.

Phoebe Tuckett (8)
St Joseph's Catholic Primary School, Haywards Heath

Quickly

Quickly the rocket blasts into space,
Quickly the multicoloured car finishes the race.
Quickly the triumphant cheetah chases the hare,
Quick is the plane but quickest of all
Is light travelling down the wall.

Charlie Kelly (8)
St Joseph's Catholic Primary School, Haywards Heath

Laughter

Laughter is multicoloured like a rainbow
It feels as soft as a dry sponge
It sounds like children playing joyfully in a park
It smells like the fresh air on a hot summer's day
It reminds me of happy, fun holidays in Barbados
It tastes like soft, smooth chocolate melting in my mouth
Laughter looks like someone enjoying themselves at a fairground.

Harry Thompson (10)
St Joseph's Catholic Primary School, Haywards Heath

Quickly

Quickly the plane rushes to the airport,
Quickly the horse gallops across the field into the distance.
Quickly the rocket vanishes into space,
Quickly the racing car wins the race.
Quickly I bounce off the waterfall,
Quickly the motorbike zooms across the road.
Quickly the train goes very fast because it is late,
Quickly the hare ran over the finishing line.
Quick is the sound, but quickest of all
Is the cheetah, that is the greatest of them all!

David Warde (9)
St Joseph's Catholic Primary School, Haywards Heath

Fun

Fun is colourful like a luscious rainbow,
It reminds me of playing in the deep blue sea.
It feels like velvet chocolate melting in my mouth,
It looks like jewels shining in your eyes.
It smells like 1,000 sweets waiting for you to eat them,
Fun sounds like a herd of elephants running at the same time.

Isabel Beauchamp (11)
St Joseph's Catholic Primary School, Haywards Heath

Anger

Stamping my feet like a bison giving its final warning,
Like it was really angry
And clenching my fists in big volcanoes of anger
About to make last explosions,
I realy wanted to let it out!
This was it . . .
The big moment . . .
I bellowed so loud
That an astronaut could hear . . . on the moon.

Sebastian Blunt (9)
St Joseph's Catholic Primary School, Haywards Heath

Laughter

Laughter is a colourful rainbow,
It feels like going to a million parties,
It sounds like music in the air,
It smells like lavender on a hot summer's day,
It reminds me of being tickled for hours,
It tastes like a huge fruit pastille,
Laughter looks like three billion pounds right in front of you!

Thomas Blunt (9)
St Joseph's Catholic Primary School, Haywards Heath

Hope

I hope I win the lottery,
I hope I own a chocolate factory some day,
I hope I ride on a steam train to a place far, far away,
I hope schools close tomorrow,
I hope I don't look like a fool,
These are the things I hope for,
But most of these things are just a daydream,
But at the end of the day these things never happen.
Please think twice about hope,
It is not a wish it is more than that,
It's charming and one more thing,
What do you hope for?

Joshua Furminger (10)
St Joseph's Catholic Primary School, Haywards Heath

A Tudor Pomander

I see the studded cloth cloves,
Piercing the silky clothes.

I smell the cinnamon spice,
It makes it smell very nice.

I feel the rough orange peel,
Making my senses reel.

Jacob Tice (11)
Tangmere CP School, Tangmere

Tudor Pomander

I see the powdery spice
It looks oh so nice.

I smell the cinnamon sweet
It smells oh so nice to eat.

I touch the pomander
That I made for Amanda.

Dominic May (10)
Tangmere CP School, Tangmere

The Pomander

I see the pomander hanging high
Just like Tudor times
I feel the spices with my hand
As they crumble just like sand
I smell the sticky luscious juice
As I pierce the skin to let the smell loose
I taste the cloves on my tongue
As their smell lingers in my lung
I hear the bright sizzling sun
I know my pomander must be done!

Alana Misselbrook (10)
Tangmere CP School, Tangmere

The Amazing Orange

I see cloves on the bare orange
as rough as a turtle's shell.
I smell spicy cinnamon
as sweet as summer fruits.
I hear the orange juice running on the skin
as slowly as a snail.
I feel rough and bumpy cloves
as rough and bumpy as a bone.

Chloe Robinson (10)
Tangmere CP School, Tangmere

The Pomander

I taste the pomander, spicy
It was cold, refreshing and icy.
I smell the heavy juices sweet
They were tied up in a ribbon neat.
I feel the pomander rough
It feels like rock that's tough.
I hear the minty cloves a-popping
Loads and loads of juice is dropping.
I see the cinnamon poured in
It looks luscious and gives me a grin.

Abbie Warrior (10)
Tangmere CP School, Tangmere

What I Think Of A Tudor Pomander

The texture is bumpy,
It feels very lumpy.

On the table it stood,
Oh dear it looked so good.

Hangs by a ribbon,
Just like a gibbon.

A Tudor pomander,
Smells like lavender.

Eve Osborne (10)
Tangmere CP School, Tangmere

Tudor Pomander

I see the studded cloves in the orange
as rough as a bit of bark off a tree.

I smell spice on the orange
as sweet as a lollipop.

I hear the juice off the orange
squirting out when I poke the cocktail stick in.

I feel the silky ribbon
as pink as a rose.

Emma Hanson (11)
Tangmere CP School, Tangmere

Tudor Pomander

I see studded cloves being poked in the orange
as hard as a stone.

I smell the golden cinnamon
as pungent as spicy food.

I hear the cocktail stick poking into the orange
as soft as a fur coat.

Melissa Killick (11)
Tangmere CP School, Tangmere

Tudor Pomander

I see the studded cloves,
Dressing the silky clothes.

I smell the pungent spice,
Which keeps away the lice.

I touch the pomander, it is round,
Which is my Earth, my world, my ground.

Melissa Hills (10)
Tangmere CP School, Tangmere

The Pomander

I see the pomander looking so sweet
It's hard for me to stay on my feet.
I smell the spices in my nose
I want to wash it out with a hose.
I taste the juice, in my mouth it's on the lose.
I feel the orange, it is bumpy,
It also feels a bit lumpy.
I hear the rustle of the bag,
It rustles like a big English flag.

Bradley Dean (10)
Tangmere CP School, Tangmere

The Pomander

I smell the orange sour,
I get a whiff every hour.
I see the bag hanging high,
Like in Tudor times.
I hear the squishy pomander oh dear!
It gets louder as I get near.
I feel the pomander bumpy,
It makes my hand go lumpy.
I taste the pomander, it is yummy,
It goes rumble in my tummy.

Nicola Frisby (10)
Tangmere CP School, Tangmere

The Pomander

I see the pomander way up high
it's about to touch the sky.

I feel the sticky juices in my fingertips
as I bite into the hard little pips.

I smell the spicy cloves
as it lingers up my nose.

I taste the bitter spices on my tongue
as it flies up my lung.

I hear a sizzle in the sun
so my pomander must be done!

Emily Clifton (10)
Tangmere CP School, Tangmere

The Pomander

I see the pomander orange and brown
As the orange is hanging down

I feel the spices with my hand
As they crumble just like sand

I smell the juices bitter
As the orange skin shines like glitter

I taste the pomander very sweet
I can't wait to have another treat

I hear the sizzle from the sun
I know my pomander must be done!

Chloe Albuery (10)
Tangmere CP School, Tangmere

The Pomander

I taste the pomander, spicy,
It was cold, refreshing and icy.
I smell the heavy juices sweet,
They were tied up in a ribbon neat.
I feel the pomander rough,
It feels like rock that's tough.
I hear the minty cloves a-popping,
Loads and loads of juice is dropping.
I see the cinnamon poured in,
It looks luscious and gives me a grin.

Danielle Foster (11)
Tangmere CP School, Tangmere

The Pomander

I see the shiny ribbon gold
As it gets so old.
I feel the squishy orange in my hand
As I throw it in the sand.
I smell the orange so sour
As I smell it every hour.
I taste the juice bitter
As I throw my pips like litter.
I hear the paper bag rustle
As around me my friends bustle.

Matthew Hart (10)
Tangmere CP School, Tangmere

The Pomander

I see the cloves are lumpy
They make the orange bumpy.

I feel the pomander as I squeeze
The juice squirts out and along comes bees.

I taste the bitter juice
As it tingles down my tooth.

I smell the strong cloves
As it lingers up my nose.

I hear the cloves crunching
As I am munching.

Leah Acott (11)
Tangmere CP School, Tangmere

The Pomander

I see the dark cloves
as brown as chocolate.
I smell the juicy orange
as succulent as an oozing jam doughnut.
I taste the orange juice
as sweet as a red strawberry.
I feel the spiky cloves
as rough as sandpaper.

Oliver Rutter (10)
Tangmere CP School, Tangmere

The Pomander

I see my pomander spiky
The pattern looks quite stripy.
I feel my paper bag it's lumpy
It looks like it's going to be bumpy.
I smell my orange linger
As I sniff my finger.
I taste the lovely orange sweet
It's a taste you cannot beat.
I hear the bubbling sour juice
It is quickly coming loose.

Tiffany Hudson (10)
Tangmere CP School, Tangmere

I Wish I Was A Pirate

I wish I was a pirate,
who sailed the seven seas
and when I reach an island,
be safe amongst the tropical trees.

I wish I was a pirate
with a parrot of my own,
I'd command all the sailors
and watch them grumble and groan.

I wish I was a pirate,
great battles I will fight,
with my scary, scarred face and my beady eyes,
I truly am a frightful sight.

I wish I was a pirate,
all the treasures I would steal,
but don't you ever cross me
or your wounds will never heal.

I wish I was a pirate,
with hair long and lank,
all my enemies come aboard,
I'll make you walk the plank.

I wish I was a pirate
and drink rum night and day
and when the journey's over,
land gently in a bay.

Emily Hill (10)
The Prebendal School, Chichester

Listen, What Can You Hear?

I can hear . . .
Lime green leaves drifting in the shadow of oak trees,
Yellow and black striped wasps playing with the busy bees.
A naughty dog annoying a horse,
The sound of the programme 'Inspector Morse'.
Your brother keeps listening to a song,
Cathedral bells going *ding, dang, dong.*
Owls are talking in the middle of the night,
Your sister telling you to turn off the light.
Cats miaowing as they always do,
A ski instructor telling you what to do.
Swans travelling in the pond,
A gun set off by James Bond.

Edward Walker (10)
The Prebendal School, Chichester

Listen, Can You Hear?

Faint ripples on a distant silky sea.
Millions of heartbeats in a sleeping city.
The soft nibbling of a caterpillar on a lonely leaf.
The quiet tapping of rain against a window.
The soft rustle of paper as you turn a page.
The scuttling of a hundred tiny legs of a centipede.
The sound of the dimming sun slipping through the clouds in
the evening.
The soft shushing of a teacher when a class is being too noisy.
The gentle scratching of my pen on pure white paper.

Polly Tyerman (9)
The Prebendal School, Chichester

In My Box

(Based on 'Magic Box' by Kit Wright)

I will put in my box . . .

A desert island shimmering in the summer sun,
The sweet song of a special cinnamon lark,
A black polar bear and a white witch's cat.

I will put in my box . . .

The tenth planet of the solar system,
The silent sound of a dragon's egg cracking
And silver smoke seeping out,
The last human being and the first dinosaur.

I will put in my box . . .

The first copy of 'Harry Potter and the Deathly Hallows',
A whiff of Montezuma's finest chocolate,
Forty winks and a blue moon.

My box is fashioned from solid chocolate and liquid gold,
With my name on the lid and my dreams in the corners,
Its hinges are made from my milk teeth which I kept safe for years.

I shall play football in my box
For the best team in the land,
I shall settle down in my box
With a wife and four boys.

Harry Dry (11)
The Prebendal School, Chichester

My Magic Box

(Based on 'Magic Box' by Kit Wright)

I will put in my box . . .

A cascading waterfall of sparkling silver
Some mouth-watering mango that will juice out your mouth
The shimmering sun streaking through the ocean

I will put in my box . . .

The tingle of the colour of magic
I can smell the Indian spices smoking up in the air
The ravishing lava spurting out a volcano

I will put in my box . . .

The glowing sunset on a gleaming horizon
Some white snow sprinkling down towards the floor
A lady, on a hot day sipping the soft touches of her fruit drink

I will put in my box . . .

A witch with a black top hat
And a magician on a broom soaring through the sky
The fresh green grass from the highest mountains

I will fashion my box out of . . .

Some velvet crunching as you wave the box
And some crimson silk spread all over the box
Pictures from a sensational skiing trip

I will do in my box . . .

Walk the wind and rain and sea
I will swim the great seven seas
Then return to my box with a soft touch.

Luciana Macari (11)
The Prebendal School, Chichester

Magic Box

(Based on 'Magic Box' by Kit Wright)

I will put in my box . . .

A lonely island shimmering in the sun,
A crunch of a perfect apple
And a pink polished pearl in the depths of the sea, unfound.

I will put in my box . . .

A marching ballerina and a graceful soldier,
A volcano erupting which is streaming cold lava
And a tree of money.

I will put in my box . . .

The first word of a baby,
The last laugh of an old lady
And a mouthful of sweet, slurping chocolate.

I will put in my box . . .

The warm smell of baking bread,
Bacon sizzling in a pan
And the sound of a train arriving at the station.

I will fashion my box out of . . .

Red rubies and sand from a hot desert,
In the corners there would be fairies whispering secrets
And the joints will be made out of dragon's claws.

I will dive in my box . . .

To see all the twirling, tropical fish,
Zoom through the fresh water
And come out all clean and new.

Maria Luc (10)
The Prebendal School, Chichester

Magic Box

(Based on 'Magic Box' by Kit Wright)

I will put in my box . . .

A sparkling waterfall flowing uphill
Succulent Turkish delight mixed with Canadian milk chocolate
And a crowd roaring at a great goal from Rooney

I will put in my box . . .

The birds'-eye view looking down on the amazing Earth
A ferocious battle between a dinosaur and the Incredible Hulk
And the delicious taste of Indian spices

I will put in my box . . .

A sip of ginger beer from Jamaica
The taste of a rare Tujamarianian peach
Soft snow melting in my hand

I shall fashion my box out of gold, snow and sunbeams
The lid shall be encrusted with stars and dragons
And the hinges, the backbone of a T-Rex

I shall fly in my box
Over the great Atlantic ocean
Land on a beautiful Caribbean beach and just relax.

Charles James-Cheesman (10)
The Prebendal School, Chichester

My Magic Box
(Based on 'Magic Box' by Kit Wright)

I will put in my box . . .

a pomegranate sunset slipping into a silver sea
a cracking sound of a leather cricket ball hitting a willow bat
and the roar of a crowd at Lords

I will put in my box . . .

a cheerful smile of my grandpa
my parents' soft voices
and my brother playing his trumpet

I will put in my box . . .

the bark of a spotty hyena
the searing screech of a laughing dog
a violent volcano spitting out blue lava

I will put in my box . . .

James Bond fighting a ferocious dinosaur
an Aston Martin being driven by a dainty dragon
and a massive mouse breathing fire through his mouth

My box will be fashioned by coal from the middle of the Earth
autumnal smoke from a bright bonfire
and the hinges will be made from crocodile teeth

I shall swim in my box; swim in all the seven seas;
swim in every corner of the deep blue sea;
up, down, left and right and see everything that can be seen.

Charlie Futcher (10)
The Prebendal School, Chichester

Magic Box

(Based on 'Magic Box' by Kit Wright)

I will put in the box . . .

The glowing orange fire of a sunset,
The sweet silver song of a swallow,
The top of the tallest trees in Tasmania.

I will put in the box . . .

White chocolate mountains with sprinkles of soft snow,
A wondrous waterfall wiping the west coast,
A brush of velvet on the smooth sand.

I will put in the box . . .

The Eiffel Tower with lava spurting from it,
A volcano in the middle of Paris,
A golden hawk watching the deserts of the Wild West.

I will put in the box . . .

A perfect breeze of a summer's day,
A desert island with a tone of treasure,
The sweetness of a patterned pineapple.

My box is fashioned from crimson silk,
Blemish-free blue paper and spotless diamonds,
Its hinges are crystal balls.

I will swim in my box, to the deepest blue sea,
To the Mariana's trench, to the bluest world.

Daniel Grimwood (10)
The Prebendal School, Chichester

I Will Put In My Box

(Based on 'Magic Box' by Kit Wright)

I will put in my box . . .

Melted chocolate with dried mango
Crystal clear water and shimmering rainbow fish
A glamorous golden eagle with wondrous wings
Dangerous rock music thudding in my ear

I will put in my box . . .

A book of imagination on a winter's night
A handful of magic which can fly me through the air
A little mouse with fire-breathing nostrils
And one dragon cuddled up in his hole

I will put in my box . . .

A sip of blue crystal water from the Caribbean
A diamond from the deepest volcano
Three silent secrets spoken in Swahili

I will fashion my box from diamond, mahogany
And oak, gold and rubies.
The hinges will be made from oyster shells
And decorated with rubies, gold and diamonds.

I will dream wondrous dreams in my box
Of heroic adventures in the far-off wilderness
Beyond the world's end.

Henry Macfarlane (11)
The Prebendal School, Chichester

My Magic Box

(Based on 'Magic Box' by Kit Wright)

I will put in my box . . .

A sapphire-blue sky from a Spanish holiday
An aroma of cinnamon and coriander
Clouds drifting past a desert island

I will put in my box . . .

The taste of mango on a warm summer night
The lost land of Limbocto
The baking of bread in a burning oven

I will put in my box . . .

The lovely lava lunging out the volcano
The perfect breeze twisting round the trees
The glint of a heavenly diamond on a dark night

I will put in my box . . .

The brush of velvet against the cushion
The glug of fruit juice on a warm morning
And the crimson silk floating against your face

My box is fashioned with . . .

The stars of the day
And the sun of the night
With the deepest dark secrets kept in the corners.

Isabelle Currey (11)
The Prebendal School, Chichester

Magic Box Poem
(Based on 'Magic Box' by Kit Wright)

I will put in my box . . .

A crystal clear waterfall shining in the sun
A soft, gentle crimson wash, hand chosen from a sunset
The sound of teeth biting through a crisp apple

I will put in my box . . .

The colour of magic drifting over the sky
The soft secrets spoken by snowdrops
The blue rippling sand and the soft silky sea

I will put in my box . . .

The lazy, light-hearted laughter of lavender
A twinkle of the first star that has triumphed over dark
The wise whispers of willows in winter

I will put in my box . . .

A scatter of clouds topped with the perfect spoon of dazzling wishes
The last ingredient that makes a potion crackle and fizz
The bitterness of chocolate and the sweetness of acid drops

My box is fashioned from . . .

Ice, coral and the most expensive platinum
With diamonds as hinges and a ruby as a latch
With secrets in its corners and dreams bursting out

In my box, I will . . .

Walk on the bluest of oceans and swim in the emerald-green grass
Sing with the birds, ride on the dolphins and play with
the cheetah cubs
I will fly over my creation, stare down at its ingredients, and smile.

Alice Tyerman (11)
The Prebendal School, Chichester

Polly's Pets

In her room Polly kept . . .
Ten little white mice scurrying around
Nine black cats with spongy soft fur
Eight slithering snakes all over the floor
Seven maggots eating all the plants
Six ducks around the colossal bed
Five kangaroos bouncing high in the air
Four parrots going wild
Three little puppy dogs chewing at the duvet
Two baby elephants waving their trunks around
One guess what? Me!

Pollyanna Hilton (8)
The Prebendal School, Chichester

Queen's dining Room

In her dining room, the Queen kept . . .
Ten long pythons that slither in the fruit bowl.
Nine great danes running up and down on the table.
Eight ferocious lions chasing her corgis.
Seven elegant unicorns sitting down.
Six tarantulas crawling on the light.
Five slow tortoises trying to sleep with all the noise.
Four orang-utans, taking the guard's job.
Three rhinos scoffing up all the food.
Two miniature pixies being very naughty.
One Queen saying, 'Bravo bravo.'

Edward Rowe (9)
The Prebendal School, Chichester

Fear Me

I am a spider that lurks in dark places
The blood that comes out of your arm
I am the bite of a shark that stings
The bang of fireworks in the sky
I am the ghost that walks around the graveyard
The shadows you see shaped like a monster.

Eve Sullivan (9)
The Prebendal School, Chichester

Sweets

Smarties, Smarties
Cakes and sweets
Yummy chocolate, lovely treats!

Herbert, sherbet yummy sweets
Where's a runny piece of treat!
There's a cheese moon in the sky
I love chocolate pie.

Smarties, Smarties
Cakes and sweets
Yummy chocolate, lovely treats!

Cuddle, cuddle my teddy bear
It's called Freddy, he is so rare
Sticky toffee and coffee
White sugar and candy.

Annabel Keoghane (7)
The Prebendal School, Chichester

Animals

Animals are stripy and some are very scary.
Animals are spotty and some are very hairy.
Animals are thin and fat, some are very small.
Animals are very cute, some are very tall.

Animals, animals lots of different animals,
There's lots of animals.

Animals are round and some are very scary,
Especially the zebra who likes to eat dairy.
Tigers are stripy, lions are small.

Animals, animals lots of different animals,
There's lot of animals.

Animals are nice to stroke,
You mustn't stroke the fierce,
Some animals are hard to see,
But some are very clear.

Animals, animals, lots and lots of animals,
There're lots of animals.

Abigail Upton (7)
The Prebendal School, Chichester

Happiness

Happiness sounds like a cello playing a jolly tune,
Happiness looks like a yellow boy running about,
Happiness smells like a freshly baked cake,
Happiness feels like a soft squishy cushion,
Happiness tastes like candyfloss in your mouth,
Happiness reminds me of a song I've long forgotten
                            and want to remember,
Happiness is joy and love mixed together.

Thomas Whyte-Venables (9)
The Prebendal School, Chichester

Anger

Anger tastes like a stream of poison has dribbled in my mouth.
Anger feels like your mouth on fire.

My heart is hot with anger.
I'm clenching my fist 'cause I'm so annoyed.

Anger looks like a bubbling volcano.
Anger feels like I'm going to explode.

Fabio Macari (9)
The Prebendal School, Chichester

Hate

Hate looks like the Devil's eyes,
Hate feels like prickles off a thistle,
Hate sounds like a piercing cry,
Hate smells like a cigarette end,
Hate reminds me of horrid things,
Hate is nasty and bad,
Hate is as common as a pigeon.
Try not to hate people,
Hate is as bad as a devil.
Hate . . .

Monty Hancock (9)
The Prebendal School, Chichester

Fear

Fear is scary,
Fear is bad,
Fear feels like you can't breathe,
Fear is when your heart is pounding,
Fear feels like you're going to die,
When you're scared you think, *am I going to die or am I going to live?*
Fear feels like someone is behind you,
Fear is when your belly is rumbling.

Christian Blagbrough (9)
The Prebendal School, Chichester

The Whispering Wind

Soft as a feather, floating off the most gentle tongue.
In a language so soft and quiet no one understands.
Colliding with leaves, whispering with the sun.
Bouncing off water and bringing with it warmth,
Murmuring with the reeds and the dragonflies.
Flying round corners and over rooftops and chimneys,
Giggling with the smoke.
Whipping round statues like whirlwinds,
The whispering wind.

Alice Sumner (9)
The Prebendal School, Chichester

Excitement

My pumping heart is pounding with excitement,
It feels like I'm big and strong.
I'm as happy as a smiling sun.
It reminds me of running like a horse through a beautiful daffodil field.
It feels like I'm prancing around,
It tastes of a brown chocolate cookie,
I've got a fantastic smile on my face.
It makes me as happy as a beautiful crystal white and yellow daisy.
Excitement is a beautiful sea with lovely calm waves.
I'm as happy as a bird singing a high sweet tune.
It smells like a sweet smelling cake in the steamy oven,
A beautiful trumpet playing a merry tune!
This is called *excitement*.

Anna McHale (9)
The Prebendal School, Chichester

Young Writers Information

We hope you have enjoyed reading this book - and that you will continue to enjoy it in the coming years.

If you like reading and writing poetry drop us a line, or give us a call, and we'll send you a free information pack.

Alternatively if you would like to order further copies of this book or any of our other titles, then please give us a call or log onto our website at www.youngwriters.co.uk

Young Writers Information
Remus House
Coltsfoot Drive
Peterborough
PE2 9JX

(01733) 890066